BY TRAIN
TO DACHAU

Printed by ETT Imprint, Exile Bay

in association with The Svengali Press 2015

ISBN: 978-1-925416-16-9 (pbk)

ISBN: 978-1-925416-17-6 (ebook)

© Renate Yates

Subjects: Raubitschek, Ernst.
Dachau (Concentration camp) – Personal narratives.
Buchenwald (Concentration camp) – Personal narratives.
Jews – Germany – Personal narratives.
Jewish dentists – Germany – Personal narratives.
Jews – Persecutions – Germany – Personal narratives.

Other Authors/Contributors:
Yates, Renate.

BY TRAIN TO DACHAU

ERNST RAUBITSCHEK

Translated and introduced
by Renate Yates

ETT IMPRINT & THE SVENGALI PRESS

For Ernst Raubitschek's grandchildren

Nicholas and Emily,

And his great grandchildren

Emma, Jock, William Ernst, Cordelia

and Thomas Ernst

Foreword

I would like to thank the staff at the Sydney Jewish Museum for their assistance in putting this book together and especially Jacqui Wasilewsky and Audrey Larsen. My thanks also to Professor Konrad Kwiet for checking my translation of my father's manuscript, and to Sally Blakeney, Rosie Block and Maria Teresa Hooke who started it all. I would also like to thank my husband Tim for his eagle-eyed proof reading and constant assistance, and my daughter Emily for her help in the book's design.

Renate Yates

Ernst Raubitschek in 1915.

A gentle man

There exists a picture of my father sitting in the garden of his parent's villa in Baden, the small spa resort just outside Vienna, a picture taken when he was 40 years old. He is blowing bubbles for me, a skinny weedy looking child convalescing after an appendectomy. The whole family used the villa, coming together on weekends, bringing children along with the usual *Kindermädchen* (nursemaids), all easily accommodated in the large and roomy house. The scene was a picture of middle class respectability and comfort. The photo was taken in 1936 – a year when one could assume that all Jews had come to terms with the knowledge of what was to come. Why did he sit apparently so unafraid, a gentle man, relying on the innate goodness of mankind. His whole life was built, so he thought then, on rock solid foundations.

The family Raubitschek of Jewish origin but not orthodox, were well respected in Viennese society by gentiles and Jews alike. They were a family of dentists who had a large well attended practice. Alfred Raubitschek, the patriarch of the family was a Kommerzialrat, as well as President of the Dental Association and also the founder of the Viennese Dental Journal. I have a large bronze relief portrait of Alfred Raubitschek showing him in profile and underneath his picture a list of his accomplishments. It is a picture of a mature, self-assured man. It was presented to him by a grateful Dental Association for his devotion and service to the profession.

In 1890 Alfred married Hermine Elkan. According to my father when they married she was a beautiful young woman with an eighteen inch waist. After the children the expansion of this wonderful waist was enormous, especially as she always ate enough for two whether pregnant or not. She was known to eat two entire bread rolls on the way home from the market said my father.

Alfred and Hermine always known simply as Mama, had four children. The eldest daughter was Fritzi, then came my father Ernst, born in 1896, then Richard and then the youngest daughter Marianne who was very spoilt said my father. Ernst and Richard worked together in the practice with their father. The equipment in the surgeries was up to date, modern and efficient which we can see from the photographs which have survived.

The children's upbringing had been uneventful. My father did not excel at school. His early school reports show a boy not exceptionally studious, probably lazy but, as the reports testify, very good at gymnastics. He was a rebellious youth and 'thrown out' as he put it himself from one early primary school. However later, at high school he began to work hard and achieved better results. At the same time he was apprenticed to Dental Studies and worked with and learnt from his father in the family practice. They had a good and well-founded relationship.

In 1915 he enlisted in the army, attended officer school and served principally in the cavalry until 1919, achieving the rank of Oberleutnant. He became an accomplished and skilful horseman and his love and knowledge of horses stemmed from that time. During his years of army service he was a prisoner of war in Italy for 18 months, where, being an officer he was treated well. He never expressed any complaints about that time. On the contrary he saw it as a positive experience and later said he had learnt a great deal from it.

On his return to Vienna, having completed his dental studies he enrolled in the faculty of Medicine at the University of Vienna and studied Physics, Chemistry Anatomy and Physiology, becoming proficient in these disciplines. He was a man with a driving ambition to learn more. Practising then, as a qualified dental surgeon, still with his father and brother he began a course in Philosophy, again at the University with a Doctorate in mind. At the same time he was also tutoring dental students in Anatomy. As well as studying and working so hard during the week, on weekends he and his friends spent their time skiing in winter and mountain climbing in summer. He became accomplished in both these sports which he enjoyed enormously.

In 1936 the unimaginable events happening in Germany were still distant and had not sounded a serious warning to the Raubitscheks. In 1934 the Chancellor, Engelbert Dollfuss, a Christian Socialist was ruling Austria as a virtual dictator who strongly opposed the Nazi Party's goal of uniting Austria and Germany. And so, by Hitler's orders, he was assassinated in July 1934. He was succeeded by Kurt von Schuschnigg who also attempted to keep Austria an independent nation.

'As I stood at the grave of my murdered predecessor, Dollfuss,' Dr. Schuschnigg wrote in his memoirs, 'I knew that in order to save Austrian independence I had to embark on a course of appeasement … everything had to be avoided which could give Germany a pretext for intervention and everything had to be done to secure in some way Hitler's toleration of the status quo.' However in the Austro-German Treaty drawn up in July 1936 there were secret clauses. In a seemingly unusual display of generosity and tolerance on the part of Hitler, Germany reaffirmed its recognition of Austria's sovereignty and promised not to interfere in its internal affairs. However Schuschnigg had made concessions which ultimately spelt doom for Austria. To quote William Shirer, "He agreed secretly to give amnesty to Nazi political prisoners in Austria and to appoint representatives of the so-called National Opposition (Nazis) to positions of political responsibility." This was equivalent to allowing Hitler to set up a Trojan horse in Austria. Into it would shortly crawl Seyss-Inquart, a Viennese lawyer, an ardent supporter of Hitler's plan. The Raubitscheks relied on the reassurances of the Austrian government that the treaty with Germany would hold and that there would be no Anschluss. These assurances diverted their attention from the real dangers which were already in the making.

Hitler was still considered unhinged, even mad, his rabble-rousing speeches hysterical and ludicrous and it was not expected that intelligent people would allow him the power he sought. In fact it was unimaginable. Nazism was an aberration it was hopefully thought, something which would run its course and then life would return to normal. Antisemitism too was not a manifest problem in Vienna – not yet that is. It was certainly there, as it always had been in the world, but underground. My mother, who was the only non Jew in the family, was the first to heed the signs. There was a family conference at the villa in Baden to discuss the situation with Mama, Papa and the brothers and sisters. Mama was by now a roly poly figure with a slight tic, a slight nodding of her head which caused the diamond drop earrings in her ears to tremble and sparkle. I still have one of those diamonds, given originally to my mother, who had it set into a ring. The family gathered around the large table in the garden where so many delicious meals had been shared. Where once, so the story went, my father's brother was laughing at his mother upon whose ample bosom sat a frog, a frog which to her horror had dropped out of a tree and come to rest there, wetly and unmoved, despite her shrieks. With mouth opened wide Richard laughed uproariously, and the frog to the family's delight, hopped into this convenient hole.

But now my mother voiced her fears.

'We should emigrate – we are Jews and the Nazis are serious – we must go.' Alfred and his wife – Mama and Papa were adamant. We are too old, Papa has heart problems but the young ones must decide for themselves. Their attitude was typical of many Jews at that time particularly older ones. My father also wanted to stay. He and the rest of the extended family rejected the idea of emigration out of hand.

'We are not criminals, we have done nothing wrong – why should we disrupt our whole lives. Admittedly there is a threat but it is nebulous – it may never happen, it will never happen.' Above all my father did not want to be parted from the city he loved. He was a passionate Viennese first – a Jew second.

My father was passionate about many things but primarily his work in which he took tremendous pride and which he loved. Mountaineering was another great love which he pursued almost every weekend in summer. In winter he and his friends skied over the many mountains in the Austrian Alps, the same mountains they had climbed in summer. These physical pursuits kept him healthy, fit and resourceful. He developed skills which later would be invaluable in his imprisonment.

He too was, a romantic. He believed with Stendhal that 'Beauty is the promise of happiness,' a saying he often quoted.

On one of his early mountaineering trips he had noticed a beautiful blonde girl waiting with friends on a railway station. He told his brother that this was the girl he would marry – a romantic idea indeed. He was a practical man as well as an optimist. He almost always accomplished what he set out to do. The first conversation between my parents on that long ago railway station concerned the borrowing of a rope necessary for mountaineering, the sport they both pursued and loved. It was enough – in 1922 they were married. Thereafter on each anniversary of their wedding my mother received red roses – as many as the number of years they had been married. They shared a love of mountains and of the outdoors and continued to live their busy and full life in Vienna. They enjoyed music, concerts and opera, still a large part of Viennese life. My mother worked at the Wiener Werkstatte, an establishment created by wealthy sponsors to help artists work at new and original designs for almost everything – for example dress and furnishing materials, silver and glassware, paper, leather goods and fashion. She designed hats, frocks, evening dresses and fantastic costumes for masked ball's one-off creations for those who could afford them. She loved her work and was a skilful and imaginative designer. My father had an extensive library. He was a collector of many beautiful art books. My mother created a beautiful ex-libris for him – a naked woman standing rather coyly on a rock. Altogether the life they had made for themselves was idyllic and seemed impossible to give up for a new and entirely unknown life elsewhere. His beloved mountains in particular would have been hard to abandon. He kept a diary of his many mountaineering and skiing trips and they make fascinating reading. A number of times he and my mother came close to death. He tells this particular story in his own words.

"One early spring a party of four of us went to the ski resort of Davos in Switzerland. On this particular morning, and in excellent weather we decided to attempt one of the runs down from the Parsenn. We took the railway to its highest point and ascended further to the Parsenn hut. From there we had a choice of many runs, most, at that great height being of quite considerable length. We decided to take the longest even though our map did not extend for its whole length. We began to ski down and, arriving at a wooden barn, saw a magnificent steep slope with the most inviting powder snow. We could not resist to ski down. At last we came to its deepest spot where we suddenly encountered a very dense wood.

We realised we had skiied off the map and had taken a wrong turn. But instead of turning back we agreed to continue along the valley and hoped to reach the railway. Unfortunately we had underestimated the length and wildness of the terrain. It was hard going and the danger of avalanches became a serious concern. We moved on and on until dark having already realised that we would, in any case, have to spend the night in the open. It was fortunate that I carried a Zdarsky tent in my rucksack. This piece of equipment consists of a sack of rubberised battist completely impermeable to water and air. It weighs little more than two pounds and thus is easily carried even on a day trip. I almost never left it behind – in this case it saved our lives. We dug a hole in the snow in a protected spot, crouched close together and drew the tent over our heads. A small piece of candle was our fire. We also took our boots off and put our feet into our rucksacks. That night the temperature in Davos was recorded at 23C below freezing. What it was in our gorge God alone knew. In the morning, rather than descend further to the river we ascended again trying to find our way out. After about twenty minutes we heard voices and there coming towards us were eight men of the local rescue team, quite surprised to see us unharmed. The schoolmaster of a small village in the environs had seen four figures skiing down towards the ill-reputed gorge where only recently a skier had frozen to death. He reported this sighting to the rescue team and after making enquiries they discovered that four tourists had not returned to their hotel that night. The team set out at dawn to recover what they assumed would be four bodies. When we emerged from the gorge with our rescuers the whole population of the village was assembled with the sledges made ready for the bodies. They were rather disappointed to see us we felt, though they did cheer when we arrived.'

There were many glorious holidays and many adventures to follow. For instance in 1925 my father and his brother Richard were very proud to have made the first climb or rather descent from the summit of the north face of a mountain called the Hochschober in the Schober Gruppe of mountains near the Gross Glockner in Austria.

The achievement of this difficult mountaineering exercise ensured their names were placed in the record books. To leave all that and his beloved Vienna behind and to start life in a new country and to change his family's lives completely, still seemed impossible to contemplate. A family so well-established, leading such satisfying lives could not possibly be in danger, or so the myth went.

Already in 1935 Thomas Mann had written in a letter, "I believe that Fascism will advance everywhere and the only question is whether Austria will be able to maintain its nuance. If it does I would really prefer to live in Vienna more than anywhere else." These were sentiments my father shared.

Throughout 1937 the Austrian Nazis stepped up their campaign in line with Hitler's ambitions. Documents were later uncovered that they planned to assassinate Schuschnigg as they had Dollfuss. But the Austrians and the Raubitscheks still relied on the reassuring words of the government.

On February 12th 1938 a meeting took place between Hitler and Dr. Schuschnigg at Berchtesgaden. At this dramatic meeting Hitler deceived, bullied and threatened the young and naive Austrian chancellor, manoeuvering him into an unwinnable position. With an overwhelming mixture of theatrical bluff and hard-nosed threats Hitler finally forced Schuschnigg's capitulation. He was presented with an 'Agreement' which in effect would hand the Austrian government to the Nazis within one week.

Schuschnigg signed. It was Austria's death warrant. On Monday March 14th 1938 Hitler entered Vienna in triumph. The Viennese, proverbial fence sitters and main chancers, lined the streets and welcomed him with raised arms and loud Heil Hitlers.

Is it a memory or did my mother tell me this story – attracted by the noise to the window of our apartment in the Gumpendorfer Strasse I stood and watched that entry into Vienna, the marching and cheering and hullaballoo. With an angry, stony face my mother dragged me roughly away from the window. It was a sight she did not want to see, her fellow Viennese with raised arms shouting 'Heil Hitler'. It was what she had predicted – it was more than she could bear. Very soon the effects of the capitulation had the expected repercussions. Neighbours began to verbally abuse their Jewish neighbours and to boycott their shops. The abuse which had already occurred in Germany soon surfaced. Antisemitism, always a fact of life but previously more subdued in Vienna emerged in full force. Jews were taunted, ridiculed and spat upon, made to wash pavements and cursed as they perforce did so. It was all exactly as it had happened in Germany.

My father was at last persuaded that it was time to prepare for emigration, time to leave. Therefore he thought it would be wise for my mother and for me to be baptised as Catholics again to facilitate emigration as well as being a form of protection. With this in mind he approached the Archbishop's office in Vienna where he was told that they would be glad to welcome his wife and child back into the faith but only on condition that he too become a Catholic. They also demanded that a new marriage ceremony be performed in the Catholic church. In the current climate, for him to be baptised was, as he saw it, a cowardly step to take and he was not prepared to take it. He would allow his wife and daughter to be baptised but he was adamant that he would remain a Jew.

He was told that these two baptisms could not be done without a dispensation from the Vatican. In the current circumstances this seemed an unnecessary and uncharitable decision. However after some weeks the dispensation was surprisingly granted. The baptisms took place and the marriage was performed in my mother's parish church without of course the usual festivities! But it was all too late.

On the 28th of May 1938 the Nazis undertook the infamous 'Judenhatz', the rounding up, quite arbitrarily, of as many Jews as they could get their hands on. My father fell into that net. Although warned by one of his patients that the Nazis were coming for him he told his brother and father to leave the practice and faced the arresting officers by himself. He describes his immediate arrest in his own words in the manuscript which follows. Then he was locked up with many unfortunate others and subsequently transported to Dachau Concentration Camp.

After this bombshell the family urged my mother to leave Vienna as soon as possible. Fortunately the relatives in England, my father's sister Marianne and her husband Ben were already prepared and were happy to vouch for us. At that time refugees were not welcomed in England. In fact they were refused entry unless financially supported. Three weeks after my father's arrest and after some difficulty in acquiring the relevant documents including Nazi passports sporting huge swastikas, we left Vienna. My mother was in tears as she farewelled her own mother, not knowing when or even if she might see her again. She was forced to leave everything behind. She never saw her beloved Bosendorfer grand piano again, nor did I ever get to use the small red skis bought for me in preparation for the next winter.

We travelled by train across what were already Nazi occupied countries and my mother remembered it as a lengthy and terrifying nightmare, a horrendous trip. The Nazi police tramped through the train demanding to see our papers and behaving with all the arrogance of new conquerors. She expected at any moment to be arrested too despite the swastika badges we wore in our lapels. Her husband having been arrested for no reason that she could comprehend except for his Jewishness, left her shattered, with nowhere to turn and no one to trust with any confidence. Now anything at all might happen to her and to me. I remember nothing of this terrible train trip although I must have been conscious of my mother's fears – a memory perhaps expunged as too frightening. I do have a hazy memory of the Channel Crossing -the sea and the wind and my mother in a deck chair no doubt feeling an enormous sense of relief. After our safe arrival in London where we stayed briefly with my uncle's friends I was taken on a ride in a red double decker bus, an exciting and in that case a memorable trip.

At last we arrived in Manchester where we were to live with Marianne and her husband Ben in their small house in Sandy Lane, Stretford. Ben had an excellent job as an engineer with the Manchester Oil Refinery. He and Marianne had moved from Moscow to England in 1937. In Moscow Ben had worked in an aircraft manufacturing plant and with more foresight than the Raubitscheks displayed in Vienna, moved to Manchester when the opportunity arose. It was a fateful move. Had they not been in England in 1938 none of the extended Raubitschek family would have been saved. As well as sponsoring us, they were instrumental in sponsoring and finding work for my two cousins Edith and Peter, the two teenage children of my father's sister Fritzi who at that time remained in Vienna with her parents awaiting, with hope, for my father's release.

In Manchester my mother found work as a dress designer, work in which she had had an excellent grounding and also, had splendid references from the Wiener Werkstatte in Vienna. There was a deal of travelling involved in reaching the factory where she worked and in her absence my Aunt Marianne looked after me. In this unfamiliar environment, listening to a language I hardly knew, she was a wonderful anchor for a confused child. Even so it did not take me long to learn English.

In Vienna, my mother with some foresight, had purchased a book for children called *Laugh and Learn English*. It was a beautiful large, red covered book with coloured pictures and both German and English underneath pictures of animals, flowers and other everyday objects. She read it to me in the mornings while we were in bed together before she went to work. Thereafter I had tried to teach my *Kindermädchen* how to pronounce 'the'. She found it quite impossible resorting to 'de' and resigning herself to my immoderate laughter. I was helped with my English too by Ericson, the son of the manager of the oil refinery where Uncle Ben worked.

Dr. Kind, indeed a kind man, would send his Rolls Royce to our modest red brick cottage to take me to his mansion (it seemed to me) to play with Ericson who was only a little older than me. I remember vividly his small record player, a machine I longed to possess. He had all the music from Snow White and the Seven Dwarfs on small records and we played them over and over – Hi Ho – it's off to work we go – and so on. Then we would sit on a rug on their very green lawn to have tea and scones. I remember that at the beginning of these outings I could not understand a word he said and then suddenly I was able to understand everything. English seemed to come quite naturally and quickly the way it often does for small children exposed to a new language.

At the same time activity intensified to recover my father from Dachau. The whole family, including those still in Vienna attempted to have him released. My mother's mother undertook a journey to Berlin where she had contacts and where she even braved a visit to the headquarters of the Gestapo on his behalf. My father's other sister Fritzi, still in Vienna with her mother, communicated with different authorities on his behalf. My mother approached the Quakers in England who at that time were almost the only organisation prepared to help refugees and Jews. Of course many letters were written – to members of parliament, to lawyers reputed to have influence, and to the various other authorities, all without seemingly any early results. Then after four months we learnt of Ernst's transfer to Buchenwald concentration camp. He was allowed to write short postcards but not to England, only to Vienna so he wrote to his sister Fritzi who sent the letters on when she could or rewrote them before sending them on to Manchester in case of censorship which was current. The Nazis did not want the fact of their concentration camps to become known abroad. These letters, precious but few and far between were at least proof that my father was still alive. But all their combined efforts to have him released seemed neverending, hopeless and without effective results.

In the meantime in Vienna, Papa, Alfred Raubitschek already ill in 1937 with heart problems, died in July 1938. His heart was unable to stand the strain of the Anschluss as well as his beloved son's senseless imprisonment. Fritzi, the eldest daughter and Mama still waited impatiently for Ernst's release.

What follows is my father's own account of his arrest and subsequent journey to the Dachau concentration camp. I translated it from the German, exactly as he wrote it.

...

Alfred and Hermine Raubitschek in Baden.

Renate and Fritzi Raubitschek.

The bronze relief portrait of Alfred Raubitschek.

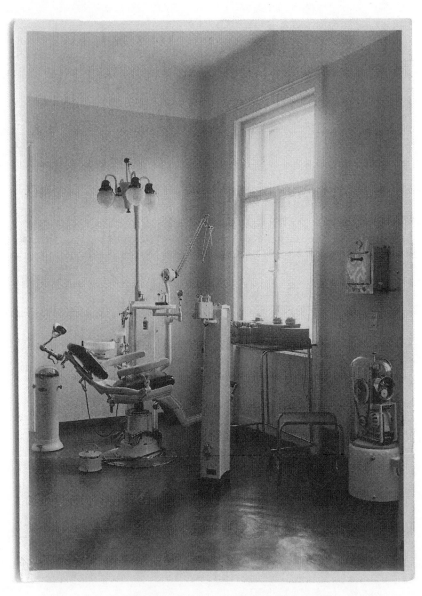

One of the dental surgeries in Vienna.

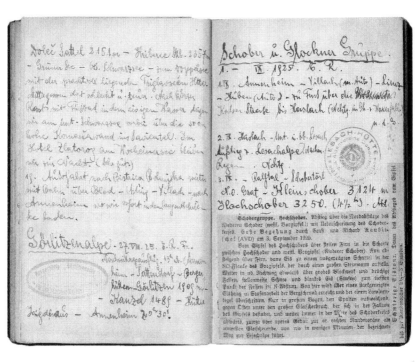

Entry in my father's mountaineering diary recording the achievement
described on pages 9 and 10. August and September 1925.

23

Eine Tür fällt ins Schloss.

Wir schreiben den 28.Mai 1938.Es ist Samstag morgens.Ganz für unser
Badener-Weekend gerüstet,mit Knickerbockers und Wadenstrümpfen,schicke
ich mich an,meine Wiener-Wohnung zu verlassen.Wegen irgend einer Lappalie
hat ein Wortwechsel zwischen mir und Fritzi stattgefunden.Die nervöse
und gedrückte Stimmung der letzten Wochen lastet schwer auf allen.Mit
dem Rucksack am Rücken gehe ich durch die ~~geöffnete~~ Eingangstüre.~~Noch
jetzt,anderthalb Jahren~~ *steht* ~~sehe ich~~ dieses Bild noch immer vor mir.Das
kleine Vorzimmer mit der Glaswand und der *offenen* ~~Ausgangs~~Küchentüre.~~...~~.

Noch einmal ~~sehe~~ sehe ich von dort Fritzi in der Küche stehen ~~und~~ mir irgend
etwas nachrufend.Wie oft werde ich mich später bemühen,diese kaum
beachteten Worte mir in Erinnerung zu rufen.Ohne Erfolg.

Dann fällt die Tür mit dem mir durch so viele Jahre vertrauten,klirrenden
Einschnappen des Sicherheitsschlosses,zu.Fürs letzte Mal in meinem Leben.
Würde mir jemand in dem Moment das sagen,so würde ich ihn für irrsinnig
erklären.

Missmutig gehe ich den gewohnten Weg in meine Praxis.Beim Margareten-
gürtel treffe ich Bruder Richard.Schweigend gehen wir nebeneinander
her.Nichts hat sich an dem gewohnten Bild der Strassen geändert.Im
Atelier ist die Arbeit samstäglich.Plötzlich kommt aus dem ersten Stock
die Frau Fritz Steiners herauf udn erzählt weinend,dass angeblich alle
Juden aus den Wohnungen und Geschäften geholt werden.Sie ängstigt sich
wegen ihres Mannes.Ich halte das Ganze für einen Unsinn.Man verhaftet
doch nur Leute die in irgend einer Weise belastet sind.Oder es wird sich
wieder um irgend eine neue Quälerei,oder besser gesagt Volksbelustigung
handeln.Man holt die Leute vielleicht wieder einmal zum Ausreiben oder
zum Exerzieren und Gelenksübungen machen.

Ich gehe zu meiner Arbeit zurück und nehme gerade einer Patientin eine
Goldkrone herunter,da stürzt jemand in mein Ordinationszimmer:"Sie
kommen schon,zu uns ins Haus."Es läutet und ich gehe sofort ins Vorzimmer hinaus.Man muss der Gefahr entgegentreten.Ein Wachmann und der
kleine dachsbeinige Kriminalbeamte,der in der letzten Zeit in unserem
Rayon Dienst macht stehen draussen.Letzterer fragt mich sofort:

A page from my father's account of his journey.

The arrest

May 28th 1938. Vienna.

It is Saturday morning. Dressed, ready for the forthcoming weekend which we intend to spend in the country in our villa in Baden, I prepare to leave the apartment. For some trifling reason my wife Fritzi and I have had a dispute. The nervous, oppressive atmosphere of these last months has weighed heavily on us all. With my rucksack on my back I go through the front door. It is a picture I see still – the small entry hall, the glass wall and the open kitchen door. Once again I see Fritzi standing there calling some last words. How often in the future would I try to recall those barely heeded words – without success. The door shuts behind me with the familiar sound of the lock snapping shut. It rings in my ears – it will be for the last time in my life. Had someone in that moment told me this would be so I would have considered him totally deranged.

With a heavy heart I make my way along the familiar streets to my dental practice. At the Margaretengurtel I meet my brother Richard and we walk along together. Silently we walk along the familiar streets together. They look as usual – nothing has altered. We arrive at the familiar door and go up to the surgeries. We begin work as usual on the patients.

Suddenly Frau Steiner comes weeping up the stairs telling us that she has heard that all Jews in the immediate area are being taken from their houses and shops and she is frightened for her husband. I assume these utterances to be pure nonsense. Surely only those who have done wrong can be arrested. Or possibly it will simply be yet another one of those vexatious entertainments they have instituted – they take people and order them to perform physical jerks or some such nonsense. I go back to my work. I am just fitting a gold crown when someone bursts into my surgery.

"They are coming – they are here – in the house." The bell rings and I go at once into the entrance hall. Danger must be confronted. Outside stand a guard and the small, bandy-legged police official who has lately done duty in our district.

"Herr Raubitschek," he said immediately, "Are you Jewish?"

"Yes I am ..."

"Then in the name of the State Secret Police I must arrest you. Is there anyone else here?"

"No."

"Do you perhaps have male employees?"

"No." Then quickly I go into the waiting room where Richard waits anxiously. "

"Disappear – and quickly" I tell him and go back into the entrance hall. The policeman is in a hurry. Later I learn that he has yet to make up the numbers of Jews demanded of him. He leaves the guard, a nice old Viennese man with me and hurries away. I go into the office, unlock the cash drawer and take some money – for whatever contingencies may happen. In the waiting room the few patients still there stand pale and shocked.

"I am ready," I tell my guardian and without hat or overcoat we leave the building. I will never return to this house – the house in which I was born, where I played as a child, where I grew up, and where for almost twenty years I went daily to work. The life's work of two generations will be simply wiped out. But I did not imagine such a thing at that moment.

The guard is ashamed. He asks me to walk a few steps in front of him. I sense how uncomfortable this whole business is for him. As we walk on I hear a nice old Viennese gentleman remark, "Good – now we'll soon be rid of all of them!"

We enter the almost bare guardroom. I am told to sit on a

rocky stool. Opposite on a bench sits Rosenrauch the local grocer, trembling with suppressed rage. Soon, the barber Glucks and then Lande the tailor from number 198 arrive. Our bandy-legged, self-important official appears and telephones the Kommissariat. Rosenrauch and Glucks, both well over fifty years old are sent home. I remember that I have some papers with me that may be better destroyed. When my sister Fritzi, pale and upset arrives with two rolls for my lunch I quickly give them to her. She tells me that brother Richard has driven to Baden to be well out of the way. Unfortunately, as I realise later, I forget to give her my keys which I have with me.

I converse with our bandy-legged official. He asks after my father and I explain that someone must work for him since he is not at all well. Graciously he allows, "we may leave your brother here to do that."

A truck arrives and we are told to get in. Already there are two other Jews and another man who clearly does not belong with us. He is wearing a swastika. It transpires he has been arrested for extortion. It seems that the master extortionists won't allow themselves be trifled with. We arrive at Hufelandgasse Police Station and are all body-searched. In particular they are looking for penknives – someone may finally lose his temper!

It is as busy as in a beehive. All the prison cells are full, even the courtyard is crowded. One meets many acquaintances. The prevailing mood is feverish foreboding, dread and yet every now and then a joke can be heard.

It soon becomes quite clear that the majority of the officials are visibly disturbed and upset by these events. One of them remarks, "We, too, know absolutely nothing – perhaps it will be our turn next."

I reflect that they too must learn and relearn from their new masters.

Gradually a friendly communication crystallises between us and our guards. Some are smuggled out and return with food and cigarettes. Together with another prisoner we ask for messages to be sent home. I put in a request for an overcoat and soon this arrives together with a large paper container. Inside I catch sight of pyjamas and immediately send the container back. Almost at once I regret the gesture. Perhaps I have refused food or more importantly a letter or some form of communication. However, later, it transpires that I did the right thing.

And now, like all the others, it is my turn to be questioned. On the printed form I see on the heading the word PROTECTORATE – I am reassured. One cannot rob wholly innocent people of their freedom for any length of time. Oh how much there is still to learn – to learn as much as one is able into the foreseeable future. The statements to be made are exhaustive. They cover everything, beginning with the grandparents and rolling through the curriculum vitae until last but not least the detailed questions concerning sexual relationships with Aryan girls and women while not forgetting the exact details of one's possessions, one's business and one's income. The gangsters are already making a profit. Only the poor people about to be plundered do not know it yet. The official who is questioning me is visibly delighted to hear that I was at the Front.

"That could possibly spare you a great deal," he says. I am not convinced. Now all the others are taken back to the cells and those who fought at the Front are brought before the official in charge. I am questioned about my four year enlistment in the army. When he hears that I was also in the infantry regiment number 84 he asks me for the names of comrades and officials. After 23 years and given the circumstances I can only remember very few. Silently he shakes his head and I am taken away. Gloomily I realise that he was probably in the same regiment and was indignant that I did not remember him despite the fact that similarly he did not remember me. Perhaps a better memory or more audacity or cheek would indeed, have spared me a great deal. I am taken back to the cells. There we hear that all those over fifty years old have been released. Steadily now, people are being taken away and transported elsewhere. I am in the last group to leave.

Together with my companions in destiny we are taken to a school in Karajan Street, which has been adapted by the Nazis to become a mass prison camp. In an upper classroom, which contains only one table, we are inspected once more. All moneys are confiscated though each man is left with ten Reichmarks. Then we are taken to smaller classrooms and formed into groups. Each group is taken down to the cellars where we are required to stuff straw into sacks for mattresses and pillows. We take them back to the assigned room where each man is given a clean, perfectly new blanket. These are clearly stolen goods – Oh forgive me, we are at war with the Jews are we not – we may call it 'legitimate booty.' We sleep three to two straw sacks, each man having his worldly possessions under his head. Outside the corridors are patrolled by Viennese security guards.

We talk long into the night. The main subject of discussion – what will become of us – what does it all mean? Gradually as in a shaken kaleidoscope a picture of the infamous May 1938 Jew Hunt falls into place.

Street by street shopkeepers were arrested. Others were contacted by telephone and asked to go to the nearest Police Station for a brief seeking of information. One was asked on the street whether he was a Jew, another had taken his dog for a walk and was never to return home. In cafes and restaurants Jews were sought out, others again were dragged out of their beds in the middle of the night. Fate even overtook some in the houses of their friends – the owner was arrested, his guests might as well come along too. Some who had business of some kind at their local police station were simply arrested on the spot. Amongst the prisoners we find a number of half Jews who were denounced by some kindly friend. On the streets and in various buildings police officials continue to ask "Any Jews around here?" And eagerly the people continue to denounce. Pointing the finger, a basic attribute of the golden Viennese heart unfolds in all its glory.

In Leopolds town whole streets are shut off and all the Jews in the area arrested. The police stations are filling up with people.

Morning comes at last. We get up, wash and then coffee is distributed. We are allowed to order necessities such as toothbrushes, soap, towels and cigarettes. Later we may purchase sausage and sweets. Although the corridors are barred we are allowed to go up into the other storeys to look for friends and acquaintances. Our main concern is to be allowed to get in touch with our relatives and we are promised that this will soon be possible.

Lunch is served – even two courses this time – soup with vegetables and also bread. Many leave the food untouched. They will soon remember the fleshpots of Karajan Street with longing. The very different temperaments are to be observed – from the highest optimism to the darkest pessimism.

At 6 o'clock dinner is brought. The overall activity reminds me of my long ago time in the military. Prisoners distribute the food and already prejudices and preferments emerge. At certain times walking in the school courtyard is permitted. There, the guards are on the whole quite nice. Since the summary dismissal of Gauleiter Globotschnig who released prisoners without consultation (what is permitted the hunter is not allowed the dog) they too are gazing anxiously into their own immediate and unknown future.

Sunday has passed rapidly. The second night is better than the first. Before we sleep some of the wisecracking fellows whose sense of humour seems indestructible raise the general mood with their wit and cause even the most intractable of pessimists to laugh and to forget, at least for a moment, the seriousness of our situation. The next day, Monday we begin to follow a routine. The straw mattresses are stacked, the blankets folded, the room swept. Benches are erected and groups come together to pass the time. Those inclined to learn even hold an English lesson. By now it seems that more of our relatives have heard of our plight. As we walk in the courtyard we can see womanly figures at the windows of neighbouring houses. They wave and make signs, attempting to communicate with the prisoners. Also behind distant curtains mysterious figures materialize. We conjecture that they have been signed up, engaged to spy and report on the prisoners and that Hitler in this way has indeed created as promised – 'work and bread' for the masses. On the pavement in front of the school a regular corso of the prisoner's relations promenade up and down, also attempting to make contact with us and soon the windows which give onto the school front must remain firmly shut despite the stifling heat.

In the evening we are suddenly given the order 'All men must immediately proceed to the gymnasium.' A large group of police followed by many lackeys enter and begin to read out lists of names. In groups of twenty they are taken away and it is quite late at night before my name is called.

Our group is made to stand in the passageway as the others are, one by one taken into the office, given their money and taken out of the building. We are the last group and even as we are called the word goes out – 'There is no more transport – this group must remain behind.' We are returned to the gymnasium where those whose names were not called are already asleep. We are given our completely cold supper and find places to sleep. I soon sleep, still unsuspecting of what dreadful adventures we have just avoided, ones the others are even now experiencing and which certainly we will not be spared.

On Tuesday we are lined up alphabetically and then placed in different rooms. Constantly we see new victims being delivered. However this manhunt is becoming more difficult. At first the unsuspecting game was easily captured. Now, frightened by events men are hiding, avoiding their own houses and all public places. In these last few days the police have gathered hardly as many as they swept into their net on the first day.

In our room I have been made Room Commander. On entrance

of State police or Gestapo people I must cry 'Achtung' and all must stand absolutely still. However our hardships are clearly mitigated by the typical usual Austrian slovenliness, and sloppiness. The Germans will be another matter – a new experience. Every day much is eagerly ordered and on suitable recompense smuggled in to us. We mingle, we walk in the courtyard, we eat, we sleep, we walk, we eat, we kill time with some boring entertainment, we eat, we sleep. The days pass. Most of us still entertain hope, some of us are able to communicate with our relations, a very few are even released. For a change we are put back into the gymnasium.

And then this night. We have prepared for sleep and are lying on our straw beds when we are rudely forced back onto our feet, into our clothes and lined up. We are about to leave.

. . .

Hell journey

Twenty men sit in darkness inside the van "Green Henry." We all gaze apprehensively through the small aperture which gives a view of the street along which we are travelling at a fast tempo. Our conjectures vary as to which police jail – Liesel or Hahngasse – we are being taken but always we hope to stay in Vienna. Now we go over the Danube Canal and onto the Ring Strasse and turn into the Mariahilferstrasse.

"So it seems we are going to the Westbahnhof after all," someone says.

Outside we see the people in the street staring at our string of motor vehicles. Inside, "Dachau?" we hear one with trembling lips murmur. Already we are entering the iron gates of the arrivals side of the Westbahnhof. Before we are allowed out of the van our guards tell us to get into the waiting carriages as quickly as we can. Outside there is pandemonium, I hear the cracking of blows and quickly put my glasses into the breast pocket of my coat and am one of the last to leave the police vehicle. The platform is overrun with German Military personnel some with rifles and bayonets at the ready. Others have revolvers in holsters at their belts in order to leave their hands free to whack us. The prisoners are lined up and then loaded into the carriages with ceaseless uninterrupted thrashings with sticks, hands, rifle butts, whips and kicks. During this mauling I notice particularly the zeal of the officers, trying no doubt to show their men an excellent example. As one of the last in our group I am lucky to receive only a kick in the shins and a rifle butt in my back.

Now we must crawl on all fours into the carriages which are German third class wagons with all the windows shut and curtained and the heating turned full on. The SS guards thrust ten men into each compartment. With the last five of our group I am hustled into the last smaller compartment with seats only on one side. I sit in the middle, to the left and right of me by chance are two Viennese acquaintances. We are given orders,

"Sit upright, heads up to look into the light, and hands on knees. No one must dare to lean back against the seat. Anyone attempting to approach the window or to look out will be shot. To speak is forbidden. To move is forbidden. And it had better not enter anyone's head to fall asleep." Constantly we hear outside the arrival of more vehicles, the cries and the thwackings of the beatings. Suddenly there is the clatter of breaking glass and we hear a cry, more animal than human, as though a pig is being slaughtered by an unpractised hand. Then a pistol shot and silence.

And yet overall there is music being broadcast, ceaselessly, to drown all other noises? We hear the departure of a train filled with children off on a holiday. They sing and shout farewells, oblivious of the events nearby instigated by the masters of their future.

It is not until it is fully dark that our train begins to move. In front of the doors of the compartments which remain shut, stand the guards. Directly upon our departure they begin to enact their well studied repertoire. Our sentry is a very young boy who warns us all once more, above all, not to fall asleep. He paints the most horrifying pictures of our punishment should we disobey him. Then he demands to know who is the youngest in our compartment. It is my neighbour (R.) on my right. Each time someone passes our compartment or enters it he must announce in a loud voice, 'Sir – here are five Jewish Schweinehunde.'

At once there must be a rehearsal, and immediately it seems the performance is not to our guard's liking. Every time the announcement is wrong or not loud enough the unfortunate declarer receives the butt end of the guard's rifle in the chest or gets a blow to the head. With his voice distorted by fear R shouts the announcement. He stutters, makes mistakes and each time receives more punishment. During the whole night there is no peace for him. When at last he manages to make the announcement correctly, tiredness or sleep overcomes him and the beating continues.

On his right by the window sits a small person, his occupation a bread hawker in the Prater. Even amongst such people there are Jews. At first he is quite cheeky and gives our guard impudent replies. He imagines that by telling the guard that he is poor he will gain an advantage. Over and over again he repeats his story and invites our SS guard to make martyrs of the rich Jews who are to blame for everything. This tactic caused him to lose his front teeth, knocked out by rifle butt blows during the night. It was only the fact that he sat by the window and was not as easily reached from the door as some others, that he was not more badly done by.

Aware of the consequences and with iron will I sit motionless in my seat. My eyes ache and tear because of the staring upwards into the light. My neck muscles cramp. It is unbearably hot. The sweat runs off our bodies and gradually our clothes become sodden. We sit pressed tightly together like herrings in a tin. In order not to become totally stiff, I constantly move my toes in my shoes. When unobserved I stretch and bend my fingers and massage my upper thighs. Tiredness overcomes my neighbours over and over again and their eyes fall shut. As often as I can I poke them with my elbows to try to keep them awake. However the hail of kicks and blows continues constantly as their heads droop and their eyes fall shut. If only we could wipe the sweat out of our eyes and off our faces.

Now a new game is instigated by our sentry. The neighbour on my left must sing a song. He begins,

'Ich habe einen Kameraden ...' He gets no further, stopped by the hail of blows which instantly rain down onto his body. How can such a miserable dirty Jew allow himself to sing a genuine German song? Now the man on my right is invited to sing. His -'Die Vöglein im Walde die sangen so wunder-wunder schön' elicits the same result. That song is also forbidden for Jews. With a broken voice and quite out of tune he attempts 'Muss i den, muss i den zum Städtle hinaus 'repeating the two lines monotonously until the order 'Enough' is given. It is my turn. I think of the childrens songs of my small daughter and sing 'Es klappert die Mühle am rauschenden Bach' which is graciously accepted. Now our tormentor wants to hear a Viennese song. Our bread hawker sings and although out of tune he sings loudly and his offering is also accepted.

In the neighbouring compartments we hear the noises of similar entertainments; shouts and screams alternating with the sound of blows and then again the singing.

Somewhere in the neighbourhood of Reckawinkel we hear for

the first time, but not for the last, the shattering of glass, then the sound of shots, and the whistling of the locomotive as the train stops. Searchlights blaze as men run onto the track, orders are shouted, the men mount the steps back onto the train carrying a burden. Slowly the train begins to move again. The slick German words 'shot while trying to escape' are heard. In fact these events occur when some unfortunate prisoner in deep despair throws himself through the closed train window and is riddled with bullets (for rifle practice?) as he lies dying or more likely, is already dead.

We have our own punishment commando who is on constant duty in our wagon. He picks his victims from the various compartments. The first is a fifty year old merchant from Meidling. He is taken into the corridor and beaten so thoroughly with a long leather whip that his screams and cries penetrate to the very marrow of our bones. And yet in our smaller half-compartment we are better off than our fellow prisoners. Above all our guard is reasonably good natured. He merely carries out orders while his comrades in their zeal cannot do enough in the discharge of their duties.

Also in the other compartments containing ten men there is not only more room but more victims. Since the men sit opposite each other there is further scope for imaginative opportunities. They must hit each other, spit on each other and kick each other. They must do exercises. One hundred deep knee bends and then with the hands held high in the air they must kneel for twenty minutes, half an hour and still longer.

And then there are party games. First the poorest amongst them must give the richest man fifty, hefty slaps in the face, the traces of which will be able to be admired for weeks afterwards. Then they change places and the richest man must do extra duty since he does not hit hard enough.

And now many of us have physical needs. In some compartments the prisoners are allowed to use their hats for this purpose – those that have not already fulfilled the need in their pants. Many are now hatless. On the floor pools of liquid form and flow slowly out into the corridor. If someone for some reason or another loses consciousness and falls to the floor this becomes an excellent opportunity to stamp on him with heavy boots until in this way he is eventually brought back to his senses.

At certain intervals the SS men are relieved by new men. This change in manpower also means a change in the amusements. With no restraints these men become ever more imaginative in their diversions until they become almost intoxicated with their work. Constantly the groans and howls of the injured can be heard, in their despair calling on God, on their parents, on their children. The more the weakest of them lose their composure the more these beasts torment them. The best and perhaps only defence seems to be a spartan attitude. In that case it seems like only half the fun.

Now the butt ends of the guns are no longer enough. Bayonets are brought into play. And again and again the windows splinter and gun fire sounds out into the night. One of the men in our carriage has committed suicide in this fashion and his corpse lies in front of the door.

Once again these monsters are working on another man whom they have pulled into the corridor. They are trying to either force him to jump out of the window or to try to tempt him to wrest their revolvers from their holsters. Despite dealing the man many frightful blows they do not succeed. He resists with all his strength and calls "Moses – help me" Immediately a revolver is levelled at his chest and fired – and with the words – 'Now let him help you' the gun is replaced in its holster. Nobody cares about the wounded man. For hours he lies there, bleeding and groaning. When he is in someone's way he is merely kicked aside or stepped over.

Suddenly someone from the neighbouring compartment flings himself onto the guard in front of our door. There is a brief struggle and the window shatters as a body flings itself out, head first with something in its hands -it is the strap of the SS man's rifle which, luckily for him snaps or the man would have been dragged out of the window with the victim. Again the guns sound, the train stops and soon the corpse is thrown back onto the train with the others.

The journey continues. Although I have remained relatively

free from persecution my trepidation in these circumstances is beyond measure. My thoughts come ever closer to the idea that it would be better to jump out of the window like the others and to try to take one of these fellows with me. Unmoving I sit in front of the brightly lit wooden wall of the compartment. This picture will remain forever in my consciousness and will become forever a symbol for me. My thoughts circle endlessly to at last grasp the resolution. When one has given up, renounced life, one looks at death with quite different eyes. It is no longer such a grave concern, such a big deal. And then I think of my wife and child and all is changed again. The earlier resolve is thrown out – I will not let go so easily. With iron determination the will to live is strengthened in me again. And all these thoughts melt into the wooden wall into an indivisible whole. In the future, in crucial moments of my life, the wooden wall will rise up before me and protect me from ill considered or hasty decisions.

Meanwhile both my neighbours have been taken out and thoroughly thrashed, with their pants down and bent over in order that the skin of their buttocks is well stretched. Now they sit on their abused parts, groaning. Sleep overcomes others. Although my need for sleep is also overwhelming I control myself and do not close my eyes even for a second. Unremittingly I maintain my position.

Later we are forced to kneel down, holding our hands high in the air. This however is a relief rather than a punishment after the hours of sitting motionless. Since we are still sitting with our overcoats on in the overheated compartment we feel the heat badly. As for the atmosphere in the compartment I do not even want to talk about it.

Outside the weather has worsened. It is raining in torrents. We should be near Salzburg by now and sure enough when the curtain is secretly pushed aside, one of us recognises the station in the early morning light.

By now a careful, mutual understanding has been reached with our tormentors. They are tired too and must force themselves to act. Only the beaters tirelessly continue to make their way through the train and we can hear the constant sounds of their whips. However, even the strength of these chosen ones begins to diminish. In order to conserve their energy they now bash the outside walls of the compartments, to make believe they are beating people and thus in the grisliest and nastiest fashion keeping us on edge, keeping our nerves taut. It takes some time for us to discover this devilish deception, some of us so far gone it is impossible to detect the difference.

Slowly the day dawns, a dull, rainy day. Our guard sits in the corridor on the heating and at last opens the door. Since many windows out there are smashed, fresh air comes in – it is wonderfully refreshing. Now he begins to converse with the prisoners and it suddenly comes to my realisation that all these middleclass existences are entirely done for, wiped out. The cliched questions begin as follows. 'What were you? What was your profession, your work? Did you have a wife? Did you have children? 'And how often must we hear the words springing from the similarly brainwashed minds. 'Why are you here? Of course because you shat on our people and fucked German women and girls.' In both these activities the Jewish people must have completely exhausted themselves!

After the excesses of the night our man seems to have mellowed. He is in a conciliatory mood. First we are allowed to wipe the sweat from our faces with our handkerchiefs. Then we are allowed to remove our overcoats and place them in the luggage rack. During this exercise he notices that our limbs have become practically useless and allows us to stand up, to move and shake our arms and legs. We also hear now that we are to be transported to Dachau. He feels the need to console us – it won't be so bad if we work properly. In that case we will also be treated properly. We will be given real beds to sleep in, enough to eat and sometimes even a piece of sausage.

The guards converse amongst themselves, drink out of their flasks and smoke cigarettes. The floor in the corridor is encrusted with a thick layer of blood and gore which ran in streams from the corpse of the man who was shot. He still lies where he fell. The guard from the neighbouring compartment, a very young fellow reaches over him to give something to our guard and in the process slips in the bloody mess on the floor. That seems to be as much as his nerves can stand. With a curse he lurches over to the window and vomits prodigiously. His breakfast sees daylight again as he continues to go to the window, over and over again even though it would hardly matter if the floor received this tribute also. His performance is accompanied by the laughter of his fellow accomplices who mock and deride him mercilessly.

The rain has stopped and from the activity amongst the SS men we realise that we are nearing our destination. Officers walk through the train, the guards don steel helmets, tidy their uniforms and make themselves ready. The train stops at a small station and carriage after carriage is unloaded.

Last night 600 healthy people with straight limbs were put into these carriages. Sixteen hours later a horde of physically and mentally shattered creatures emerge from the Dachau Express. Many can only alight with help from their comrades. Heads are covered in blood, teeth and eyes are bashed in, bones have been broken – overnight a huge number of people have been reduced to cripples.

But nothing must be overlooked. The three dead from our carriage must be taken out. With three others I carry one of the corpses. It is the body of a strong, sturdy middle-aged man. In our exhausted state the burden seems terribly heavy. One of his legs has been completely shattered and hangs down, only connected to the body by bloody skin and muscle. Soon our hands resemble butcher's hands and our clothes are stained with blood. On a nearby track stands a short goods train consisting of three enclosed cars and one open one. The corpses are gathered together on this last, and we too, panting and gasping, throw our burden up amongst the others.

The whole area is encircled by guards who are armed to the teeth, and now we are pushed into the other three empty cars – 200 men in one car! Many must be lifted and forced in. The ventilation louvres must remain closed. Every attempt to open them is rewarded with gunfire. The doors slide shut and we are in darkness. Some friends find each other, we try to make more room for the more severely wounded and one group has got together and we hear the murmur of prayers. In corners and against the walls those who have restrained themselves for so long relieve themselves and soon the cars are dripping – no upbraiding from outside can stop the flood.

The wheels begin to turn and their sound blends with the noises of groaning and sobbing, the loud praying and now other conversations. One comforts the wounded and is in the circumstances happy to be able to speak at all. The airlessness of the confined space now makes itself felt. Many become ill, some vomit and there is frightful confusion. Someone carefully opens a skylight without being detected but the meagre fresh air that is allowed to enter is simply not enough to freshen the foul atmosphere. And the engine whistles constantly in a ghastly manner – a sound which also remains forever in my memory.

With a jolt the train stops. Everyone tumbles together. The doors slide open and the pathetic contents of the stinking wagons pour out onto a flat tract of land covered in huge puddles of water. On one side there are groups of pine trees, on the other side stand wooden barracks. We learn later these are military quarters. Once again the whole area is surrounded by heavily armed guards. Those nearest the wagon doors attempt to deliver some last kicks and blows to those emerging. We are now hunted hither and thither through the rain puddles, no one knows why or where.

We are to stand in rows of four – I should say an attempt is made to stand us in rows of four and still there is a muddle. Fear and trepidation has transformed this group of men into a headless herd of sheep. All try to crowd into the centre, one treads on the fallen almost as a matter of course. One pushes and is pushed and always the weakest ones come off worse. Involuntarily I am reminded of those American films in which great herds of cattle or sheep are rounded up – the sight is so similar that one could believe it is animals that are being dealt with here. Do we do the animals an injustice when in these circumstances we blame them for being illogical, unreasonable, without reason? At last a kind of order is reached and I stand in a row of four in a puddle. Suddenly, in the row in front of me there is a stirring, a disruption. In the next minute the figure of a man in a beige trench coat appears to take a few steps towards the pine wood, bending low as though for cover but instantly there is the sound of machine gun fire and he sinks to the ground as though struck by lightning. There are others who drop to the ground as well and there are some screams from those also caught in the crossfire. Later we discover what actually happened. The dead man was the son of an Austrian linoleum manufacturer and had in his possession an American visa. Despite all his protestations he was arrested, like so many others, and put on the transport to Dachau. The unlucky man was attempting to change his fate in a last minute protest which he indeed succeeded in doing but not as he would have wished. When he complained he immediately received a number of fists in his face and as he instinctively tried to avoid the blows took the fatal steps. It was the moment those beasts were waiting for – an excuse to satisfy their murderous proclivities. In that company those who have not yet killed someone are not of the hierarchy. The result of all this we already know, however there are others who are also wounded. The incident cost a youth from Meidling his leg. An SS man received a bullet in the stomach and some days later we deduce with a great deal of satisfaction, from the flag flying at half mast that one of these murderers has succumbed.

To conclude our trip we are made to run a veritable gauntlet over about 1000 metres. We are hounded along at a fast running pace through puddles and dirt and with the soldiers who border the way doing their best to inflict further brutalities upon us. Now the path becomes a sealed road and we can see a building in the distance. It is a long single storied structure with a kind of high tower in the middle. As we approach we see that the broad entrance leads under this tower and through the middle of the building. We feel that this is our destination and hurry towards it with the last of our strength. We hardly hear the curses flung at us, we hardly feel the kicks and rifle butts on our bodies. Forward is the watchword with no consideration for the sick and weak. Some fall down, others fall over the fallen since every delay is bound up with more fear.

The herd is driven through the entrance and a sigh of relief whispers through the ranks for the German heroes must remain outside. The strength leaves some of us and others, totally exhausted, drop to the ground unconscious. Bringing up the rear of this unhappy procession is a long row of stretchers.

Then the iron gates shut – on them we see the words 'Arbeit macht Frei' fashioned in delicate, wrought iron letters.

…

In Dachau gibt es nur Gesunde und Tote

In Dachau there are only healthy men or corpses.

It is now later in the morning. We are driven through the gate and turned to the right, where we are again made to stand in rows of four. We stand. It is the first lesson in standing, an important requisite of camp life – that carefully thought out system of further torment for us. We are standing in front of a long building still under construction. Constantly we hear the noises of sawing and hammering and the shouts of the carpenters. How dearly I would like to do the work of these carpenters and yet how different it was to be.

Slowly, and with the returning of a kind of peace, I begin to examine my surroundings. In front of us runs a broad track, then there is a 3 meter high wire abatis and beyond that a wide trench filled with swiftly flowing water. On the other side of the trench stand many low buildings. Not only on the entrance building, which is the so called 'Jourhaus' but also on many points of the surrounding fortifications stand high watch towers. These are manned by guards with machine guns who are entertaining themselves by turning their guns towards us and practising their aiming. Aeroplanes constantly circle above us and over the camp.

The sun breaks through the clouds and gives us some much needed warmth. Now and then minor officials, armed only with pistols come past dealing out various orders – comrades must be supported – but at the moment we are spared violence. If only hunger were not making itself so strongly felt. Again, here and there exhausted men collapse. No one may touch them, no one can help them.

Suddenly a robust young boy rolls convulsively on the ground, blood red in the face and as suddenly lies still. A hefty kick helps him to his feet but he immediately collapses again. The bayonet stab he subsequently receives leaves him in the so called 'field hospital' for six weeks.

After more hours of standing the whole herd is gathered together on the large square, the rollcall site, in front of the 'Jourhaus.'

The primary camp leader Sturmbahnführer Koegel who looks like a jovial mixed business grocer, holds a short lecture.

"You now find yourselves in the concentration camp Dachau. The first command is absolute obedience. Any, or even an intimation of resistance will instantly be broken. You have already had a taste of this on your outward journey. If anyone has a mind to escape just let him try. There is the wire – it is electrified. You men will soon see how the steam and smoke flies out of the fellow's arsehole. If you behave yourselves, nothing further will happen to you in this camp. However the slightest transgressions will be heavily punished and every such punishment will lengthen your imprisonment by six months." With the prediction that we would now be given something to eat he leaves the square. But we must endure our gnawing hunger and above all our frightful thirst for a while longer. We are, as is said in the camp, 'stuck with the underling' and this underling is Sturmbahnführer Grunewald 2 L.F. who is in charge of these regulations and it seems in his eyes that there is still plenty of time for our repast.

In smaller groups we are taken out through the gate to the barracks housing the political division of the Gestapo where our reception takes place. We are shaved, all personal details are noted beginning again with our grandparents and ending with sexual conduct with Aryan women. Every one of us receives a prison number and is photographed from three sides. Even our fingerprints are not forgotten. While others are thus inducted we must stand with our faces to the wall, immobile. Talking is forbidden. It is now afternoon, the sun burns down and yet hunger and thirst drives out tiredness.

The troop is taken back into the camp where we are ordered into an empty barrack house. In the large room many tables are set up at which sit various officials. Our accompanying Block leaders (underofficers of the camp administration) are amazingly magnanimous. Only with their gloves do they hit us in the face, or bash us on our heads with their thick notebooks. I will no longer mention the occasional box on the ears because this is simply part of the daily bread of the camp life.

First of all any foodstuffs people have, or cigarettes and so forth are collected and thrown into rubbish bins. Then anything else we have on our persons must be taken into our hands, then all our pockets are turned inside out. With hands held high we are moved towards the main door where the Block leader searches us from top to toe. At the first table our belongings are taken from us. We are allowed to keep handkerchiefs, money purses containing 5 marks, braces and spectacles. Everything else is retained. Then our clothes and shoes must be removed and are placed in numbered sacks by older prisoners. We stand there, stark naked, ready for the Doctor's examination. Now on our naked bodies the signs, the traces, the marks of the previous night become truly visible. To my amazement every mark is recorded with German efficiency. Perhaps one day these German cultural records will fall into the right hands! There is no place on the human body that has not received a wound, some more serious and some less serious.

However the words most often inscribed on the reports are – 'Haematoma on the Posterior.' Simple words that anyone who has seen them do not do the horrifying bruises, blisters and wounds, proper justice.

Every disease, and not only those suffered by the prisoner but also by his parents, is fully noted down. All operations, childhood diseases and even psychiatric problems are all noted. Thus statistics on race and heredity are collected. Our bodies are measured and even weighed and so it is that many of us discover how it is possible to lose 5 to 6 kilos in one night.

As an outward sign of our imminent slavery the hair on our heads must now fall, and since we cannot remain naked we must be clothed. It happens very quickly – 6 pieces of clothing are pressed into our hands; a pair of roughly sewn and nailed pair of leather shoes, 1 pair of woollen socks, one shirt, one blouse, one pair of trousers and a cap made of new grey and dark blue striped cellular woven wool. On the left breast and on the right trouser leg shines a magnificent Star of David created by two triangles, one of red, one of yellow – yellow for the Jews, red for the political prisoners.

Time passes. We are taken outside again and then allowed almost two minutes in a warm bath in order to rinse off the worst of our dirt, blood and sweat. It will be our last bath for three months. Still wet we climb into our new clothes. Some dawdlers are helped along by slaps to the legs and at a run we are returned to the *Jourhaus*.

More examination of our personal details – there is method in this repetition. Perhaps a prevaricator will make a mistake and thus be caught out.

Troops of weatherhardened prisoners pass us by with strange rhythmic strides, singing as they go. Their clothes are marked with coloured stripes, faded by weather and sun and have sewn on them many curious badges.

We stand and wait in the large courtyard and see also standing at the gate, a number of odd immobile figures, their faces turned towards the sun. Sometimes one of them falls to the ground. No one looks at him. Then wearily he raises himself, obviously happy that no one has noticed him.

One prisoner, clearly in a superior position, mans the gate as there are constant comings and goings. The SS people have bicycles with which they conduct their business, inside and outside. New prisoners move about the square, always at a trot.

A strange vehicle also attracts my attention. It looks like the trailer of a two ton truck but has shafts. It is being moved by human strength. At the sides they are connected by ropes and wooden halters and at the back too. The prisoners drag the wagon, panting and sweating and constantly at a trot.

It is the infamous 'Dachhauer Moorexpress.'

The sun goes down and evening is beginning. We wait and stand and stand and wait. It is night. At eleven o'clock it is finally our turn. We march into the camp to block number XVIII. One hundred men are put into a space meant for fifty. Each of us is given an aluminium plate, a cup and cutlery. A few of the younger ones must fetch the food while we sit on the floor where we stood before, each of us holding his eating utensils almost convulsively fast in anticipation of the meal. At last towards midnight we receive a soup containing pieces of meat and vegetables as well as some bread. The picture of the eaters sitting around on the floor is indescribable – it is our first mouthful after 30 hours without even a drop of water.

On the floor of the sleeping room straw sacks have been laid out – two for three men as well as two blankets for each man. The flock sinks into a deathlike sleep filled with the wildest of dreams. The first test of the performance abilities of our bodies has been withstood. But how many have succumbed on the journey and how many will perish as a consequence of this same journey?

And what fate awaits us all? The snoring of some of the sleepers resounds loudly through the room. Here and there a figure clad only in his shirt slips outside and later, relieved, returns to take up his place again. Curses are heard when one of these men inadvertently steps on a sleeping comrade – an incident often repeated, often since we have hardly room to move.

The noises of the sleeping human herd combine with the groans of the wounded and the cries of those dreaming.

We go forward towards an unknown tomorrow.

An incident took place three weeks before we were transported to Buchenwald.

The various Arbeitskommandos, that is work-commandos, fetch people from the various blocks. From time to time some of the prisoners remain behind. Clearly there is not enough work to hand and not enough SS people to plague the leftovers. However sometimes even the lucky ones left behind are forced outside to do knee bends and various hour-long strenuous exercises.

After roll-call the larger commando groups are put together first. Then the smaller groups are collected together. These are often composed of only three, four or five men. On the day this incident takes place I am on the borderline of being chosen or not. Today we deduce that probably almost half of us will remain behind. We always put the weaker and sicker ones of our lot into the rows at the back so that they will be spared from being forced to go out to work. Just before my row is called the last group is marched off. Then an older, surly looking Kapo arrives and demands six men. Because of this sixth man a debate takes place and finally a German Jew from another block volunteers to be the sixth man. I too am one of the six.

It is incredible how often our fate depends on pure chance. We are marched off and receive two SS men as guards. As we are all new to this commando group we try to guess whether the day will be just normally bad or perhaps much worse. We pass the gate and are marched along the length of the camp road right up to the furthest end of the SS quarters. The tempo is bearable and we imagine that today will not be too bad. At last we arrive at a small barracks where we are given a hand cart and made to load it with various building materials. We go on. We pass the porcelain factory, cross by the SS riding school at the very end of the camp and unload our materials at a small hut. Here the notorious Dachauer Swamp begins and we see a group of workers standing up to their hips in water. We are given spades. An SS man tells our Kapo that first the road must be levelled. Rain and trucks have left the sandy road in a deplorable condition and we must make it serviceable again. Immediately the two guards begin their customary harassment. Since we are only six men it is much more unpleasant than in larger groups. Our every action is criticised, we are constantly driven, threatened and even rifle butts and bayonets are used. Our Kapo who is in fact an anxious type of person, naturally does not want to be 'noticed' and even surpasses the guards with his tormenting. Fortunately the road is levelled in about two hours as we could not have withstood the tempo any longer. We go back to the hut, retrieve the hand cart and proceed to the edge of the SS camp Riding school.

Large heaps of building materials from barracks that have been demolished are lying around. First we must clean the beams and rafters and remove endless numbers of rusty nails. Then we load the hand cart with as much of these materials as it can hold. We go forward with a load which on a normal road would only just make it. When we reach a sandy patch the wheels sink into the dirt and we can hardly move forward at all. Sweat runs in streams down our faces and backs. Even the Kapo must help and the guards try everything they can to drive us forwards. It reminds me of scenes when in the past, horsedrawn vehicles were similarly stuck in mud and everything was done to free them. And so we go forwards slowly, sometimes merely a metre or so, sometimes a little more. The work is so hard even these beastly brutes call for a rest. At last we are in sight of the prisoners working in the swamp water. A field railway leads to the place.

The whole of the workplace is surrounded by a thick chain of guards, since in the swamp, weeds and thickets are good hiding places. In one part, quite close to the guards there lies a heap of boards and posts. We take some of the material from our cart and carry them to the heap. Then, since there is no more room on this particular heap our Kapo directs us to make another heap a few steps further on. One after another we throw our burdens onto this heap.

I have gone about fifteen steps or so back to the cart when I hear the crack of a rifle shot quite close to me. Immediately we hear the order 'Everyone down' and a siren begins to howl. I throw myself to the ground where I stand, my face presses into the dirt. We can see nothing as it is forbidden to look up. We hear shouts and curses. In any case I enjoy the enforced and unforeseen rest. The smell of gunpowder is in the air and we lie for about fifteen minutes on the ground. Then the SS Underofficer on duty appears on a bicycle. This raising of the alarm shows that despite the miserable condition of the prisoners, the administration of the camp is in control and to be feared.

It turns out that the new place where our Kapo had told us to throw down our loads was about one pace outside the ring of guards. The nearest guard woke up to this fact after five of us had left to return to the cart, he then fired on the last one of us, the sixth. He is the German who had willingly volunteered for duty this morning and was about to throw down his load when fired upon. Wounded, the man fell to the ground and no one was allowed to touch him until the duty officer appeared.

The man is not mortally wounded and he moves and even speaks. We remaining five receive the order to march. Our kapo is visibly upset. He knows of course that he is to blame for the whole affair, quite apart from the stupidity or maybe even sheer vindictiveness of the guard who fired. He mutters constantly and is clearly struggling to find a way to foist the blame onto someone else. Since we five are the only ones available, and despite the welcome interruption of work, we are none too pleased. We arrive back at the camp and must take up our places, standing near the gate on the roll-call square. Fearful and terrified beyond measure, the swine of a Kapo runs up and down in front of us. In spite of his obviously evil nature he is too stupid to find the right way out. Along comes Sterzer to rescue him. He is somehow connected to this man Sterzer, a multiple murderer long before the Nazi time and now head Kapo, Oberkapo of Dachau. Excitedly our Kapo falls upon this fellow, his accomplice and in whispers informs him of the facts and of his anxiety in case of an investigation; for the Nazis with their devilish methods love to punish the very prisoners they have put in charge of the other prisoners. Whenever an opportunity arises they put this method into practice and punish the Kapo who is also somehow at fault, in the most ruthless way possible. The two accomplices soon understand each other and Sterzer's tip soon becomes clear to us. Sterzer comes over to us and declares loudly,

"So... the Schweinehunde won't work eh? Put them on immediate report for refusing to work. We will show these bone lazy bastards – report them immediately." Already he takes paper and pencil and instructs our Kapo at least three times,

"Reported for laziness at work – we will show you soon enough." Much relieved our old idiot takes down our names, numbers and block numbers.

The whole exercise is completely clear to us and goes as follows;

1. Intimidation, in case the commando group should initiate an investigation.

2. Diversion of the whole shooting episode.

3. In case anyone speaks out against him the Kapo can say,

"They wouldn't work and now they want to revenge themselves on me.

It is all lies."

Thus the twisted discipline of Dachau.

The man who was shot died soon afterwards. And as for me, had I been the sixth man these lines would never have been written.

...

My father's manuscript ends there. He wrote no more but spoke, albeit reticently, about his further experiences and I remember very well the few he did tell. Because I did not discover the manuscript of the terrible train journey until after his death I was not able to ask him why he did not continue the account of the remaining months of his incarceration. I can only surmise that he did not want to relive any more horrors. He was transferred to Buchenwald in September 1938. What follows are his experiences in that camp and those of innumerable other Jews, many of which have also been documented elsewhere. He told me many of these over the years.

...

Buchenwald

The concentration camp Buchenwald was situated in a large beech forest on the Ettersberg Plateau near the town of Weimar. It seemed an unlikely site for such a camp, so close to Weimar, so famously associated with names such as Goethe, Schiller and other people closely linked with German culture. Goethe was said to have described the Ettersberg as 'a place where one could feel great and free.' An irony indeed. The camp was very much larger in extent than Dachau. There was a barbed wire fence around the whole complex. At measured intervals, of which there were many, watch towers loomed, manned by soldiers wielding machine guns. The camp was constantly being extended as more and more unfortunate people were arrested.

Many were still detained for political reasons, such as communists and other dissidents as well as Jews and homosexuals. Prisoners were not allowed into the beech forest and the building extensions except during working hours. The undergrowth in the forest had been so stamped down by the prisoners' boots that not one blade of grass had survived. Therefore in this strange forest there were no insects nor even any birds amongst the trees. No bird song, no sounds at all. It was an eerie place and reflecting the prisoners expectations – seemingly an entirely hopeless environment.

The journey from Dachau was unremarkable though perhaps I should say remarkable in that it was more or less without the foregoing incidents on the train to Dachau. The prisoners were even given bread to eat on the journey in the train and allowed to visit the lavatories. On arrival in Weimar they were hustled off the train and loaded onto trucks the interiors of which were in darkness. Orders were to bend down, head between knees and remain so. All they were able to ascertain was that the journey was uphill. After being unloaded the formalities of admission were executed. Their belongings, such as they still had, were taken from them but they were allowed to keep a certain amount of money. Also my father was allowed to keep his spectacles. As usual the German need for tabulating and making lists caused this process to take a long time. The endless standing took its toll of some of the older and feebler men who, when they collapsed, were beaten mercilessly as were others who tried to help the weaker ones. Finally the prisoners reached their barracks and were placed in dormitories – 200 in a dormitory meant for 100 and with the same sacks filled sparsely with straw for beds. They were given nothing to eat. My father's new life here began with the gnawing hunger he would experience over the next months as his constant companion.

The day in Buchenwald began with the first roll-call, there being another in the evening. The morning call took place at 6 am, the other at 4.pm. The prisoners were ordered to march to the square where they were counted by the barrack orderlies who reported their numbers to the barrack officers who reported to the roll-call officer who added up the figures and reported to the commandant. A cumbersome system which worked reasonably well in the morning but came to grief very often in the evening when some prisoners were still at work in the outside gangs. Finally, when the numbers were correct, the loudspeakers would bawl out the names of the prisoners who had been reported during the day. Justice in these cases was swift. The usual punishment was twenty-five strokes and the floggings took place on the spot. As the floggings went on and on not only every blow but also the moans and cries of the victims could be heard. It would always take a long time until the prisoners were dismissed and at last allowed to return to their barracks. In Dachau the roll-call served chiefly to count the prisoners. In Buchenwald it was used by the commandant and his aides to play the tyrant over their 10,000 slaves. Commandant Roedl was an SS officer of about 40 years of age with a flabby face and a fat body. He was said to have started life as a mechanic and when the Nazis rose to power became the owner of a brewery. He was regarded as a drunkard and obviously was one. He was very quick-tempered and often thrashed prisoners with his own hands. However in most cases of disobedience or insubordination he took the victim's number and had him punished at the evening roll-call.

In Buchenwald the men were stacked into barracks. Each barracks was divided into two sections – the dormitory and the mess. The prisoners slept on the floor on the usual straw sacks – two to three men and a blanket each. After some weeks they were given beds which had to be made tidily in the eyes of the orderlies. When beds were not tidy enough and difficult to accomplish because of the ragged and tattered bedding, punishment followed for the whole dormitory. In Buchenwald the whole community was made to suffer for the 'crimes' of the individual. Punishments were ingenious. For instance one night the prisoners were awakened by a loud order from their barrack orderly, "Get up and get dressed immediately.' It was the middle of the night, the first time this had happened and the feeling amongst the prisoners was that something was badly wrong. Everyone was very frightened by this unusual occurrence. They did as they were told, then were lined up and marched to the barrack square. There in the glare of searchlights they were lined up again and told to stand and wait. Two hours later came the voice of the commandant over the loudspeaker, 'Prisoners – you will soon see the corpse.' It was only a death in the camp – they had feared it would be something far worse. It had occurred to my father that perhaps Hitler had been assassinated and therefore the SS would do terrible things to the prisoners on account of it. However soon two barrack orderlies appeared carrying a body on a stretcher. Out of the loud speaker came the voice again, 'There is the miserable criminal – look at him, look at his corpse and remember him well. That is what will happen to all those who attempt to force their way through the barbed wire. And now dismiss.'

Cold and shivering the prisoners returned to their barracks. It was a cruel exercise in power – to rouse ten thousand men in the middle of the night, keeping them in suspense and fear for a couple of hours before showing them a dead body.

This incident however did not exhaust the devilish ingenuity of the camp officers. One day the barrack orderlies and gang leaders reported more prisoners than usual. But these criminals were not flogged that evening as had always been the case.

The following morning they were lined up and marched into the forest. The thirty-five prisoners were hanged from some of the many beech trees by their hands. The pain was unimaginable of course and their groans and screams resounded throughout the forest. The mightiest tree in this forest, the Goethe Oak stood not far from this scene of horrendous torture, the same tree where Goethe often sat dreaming and composing his immortal works.

A curious phenomenon in Buchenwald was the fact that the camp was to a considerable extent ruled by the 'green' prisoners. These had been professional criminals outside the camp and formed a kind of second administration. Many of the barrack and room orderlies as well as many of the work gang leaders were 'green' and so were the majority of the supervisors who deputized for the barrack officers. They moved between the labour gangs and between the barracks in search of victims whom they then reported, unless of course they were paid off. These criminals wielded a certain power not only downwards but upwards. Some barrack officers were obviously as thick as thieves with one or other of the 'greens'. This close association of the SS with ordinary criminals was significant. The commandant made two attempts to break the power of this second administration but failed. Their link with the barrack officers was too strong. Therefore there was corruption everywhere in the camp – in the registry, the post office, the kitchen, the canteen, the clothes store, the workshops, the labour gangs and the barracks. The upper limit of this system must have been very deep rooted to subsist despite the commandant's actions. All this would have been quite impossible in Dachau. One prisoner put it thus, 'Dachau is a bestial but rigidly organised penitentiary. Buchenwald is organised gangsterdom.'

Work in Buchenwald was organised by dividing the prisoners into labour gangs. Sometimes one hundred to a group, at other times merely half a dozen depending on the work. Special jobs were frequent. One of these jobs was to move huge tree trunks away from the forest. This was all part of levelling the terrain for further buildings. There were plenty of men available but the guards always seemed to choose as few as possible so that the prisoners were hardly able to lift and move the load. This inevitably caused much mirth amongst the guards who merely increased their threats and curses until the task was, with difficulty, accomplished.

In the barracks some prisoners were detailed to do the day to day work such as washing eating utensils and attending to so called 'untidiness.' These men were not required to work outside and remained in the barracks during the day, careful to keep out of sight of the guards who might nevertheless send them out to work. To be on inside duty was a terrific advantage and many prisoners paid a great amount of money for the privilege. It meant rest, important as they worked for only about two hours a day. It also gave them a certain amount of power. These men were hand in glove with the barrack orderlies and made money by smuggling and other nefarious activities, all at the expense of the other prisoners. They could have done a lot to relieve their comrades' suffering but were generally unfeeling and tough. It was every man for himself in this hell on earth.

Mail in Buchenwald was severely restricted. That any correspondence at all was allowed was in fact surprising. Prisoners were able to write and receive two letters per month, always supposing no punishments were in progress. Punishments meant no correspondence into or out of the camp, often for a month or more.

Lined paper and envelopes or sometimes small postcards were provided. One of these was received by my Aunt Fritzi in Vienna and is shown on page 73.

There were detailed instructions for the writer, written in red. In the main, orders were for the writing to be absolutely legible, the writing to stick to the printed lines and, under no circumstances, was any writing to appear in the margins or anywhere else outside the lines on the paper. If these orders were ignored the letter or card would be destroyed. In fact the word used on the card is 'vernichtet' a horrible word which also means 'annihilate' – the word constantly used by Hitler when ranting about the annihilation of the Jews. Further orders issued were that nothing that happened in the camp was to be recorded, neither was the question of the prisoners release or any illness or injury he might have sustained. Prisoners were all supposed to be supremely well

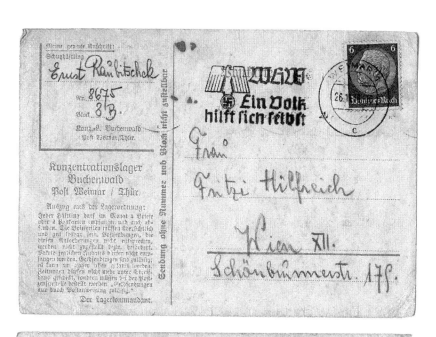

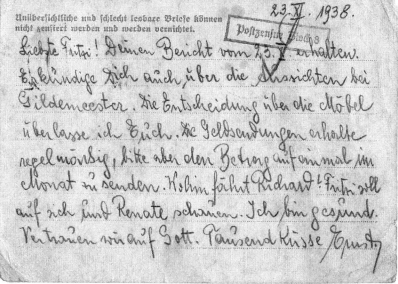

My father's postcard to Aunt Fritzi from Buchenwald.

and in good spirits. The only subjects permitted were arrangements for emigration out of Germany and requests for money which when sent was paid into the prisoner's account. Families were supposed to think that conditions in the camp were ideal since there were no complaints. One request my father made was for new spectacles to be sent as his had been broken – this was allowed through the censor. Needless to say no letters were permitted to be sent abroad. That is why my father wrote to his sister Fritzi in Vienna and she rewrote the letters in case of censorship and sent them to my mother Fritzi in Manchester. Another request my father made to his sister was as follows –

'Please send Fritzi, 16 red roses to reach her on 15th December.' That date was their wedding anniversary and 16 the number of years they had been married.

At that time in Buchenwald there were still efforts at a kind of normality. Along one side of the barracks square was a long alley which was fenced off with non-electric barbed wire. There was a smithy, a sawmill, a cabinet works, a bootmaker, a tailor's shop and a canteen. After the working day prisoners could avail themselves of some of these facilities. All the workers were prisoners who had the advantage of working undercover and much illegal trading went on amongst them. For instance cigarettes were always available either from the canteen or from other prisoners or orderlies and could be resold to others. The canteen, where bread, sausage and sugar were also available for a price was often closed because of some punishment or other and so prisoners continued to starve since the rations provided were inadequate consisting of watery soup or stews with little real nourishment. A feature of prison life was the bastardry of the barrack officers who brutalised the weak and caused much havoc with ingenious and malicious punishments connected with such food as was available.

At one time the deficiency of vitamins in the food was suddenly addressed by the authorities. It was announced that henceforth the prisoners would receive extra rations containing vitamins and stressing the importance of vitamins. What they received was an extra spoonful of raw cabbage and some sausage but after a few days the new rations were suddenly stopped. Everything in Buchenwald was contradictory and absurd. One explanation of the vitamin fiasco was that mortality in the camp had surpassed the statistical limit and such statistics must be rigidly observed. The Nazis loved order above all.

I could list further bizarre episodes and atrocities but enough has been said and recorded in the past. I can at least tell one story of my father's which had a happy outcome.

In November 1938 he was working on one of the building sites which was destined for barrack buildings to house more prisoners. Owing to his ill-fitting boots a blister appeared on one of his heels. The blister became larger, did not heal and eventually became infected. My father with his knowledge of medicine realised that the high temperature he had as a result of the infection was a sign of septicaemia – generalised blood poisoning, a dangerous and life threatening condition. He made his way to one of the two hospital buildings hoping for admission. The hospitals had about 130 beds for the 10,000 prisoners in the camp, many of whom were continually sick owing to the inadequate diet or injured as a result of being beaten and otherwise physically maltreated. Often men had to be satisfied with a bandage or some simple medicine administered by an assistant first aid man. For men suffering from stomach or other intestinal afflictions there was only one medicine –.castor oil, and this for men already suffering from diarrhoea! In my father's case, luck or destiny prevailed. He was admitted to the hospital and examined by a Doctor – a German Aryan Doctor who diagnosed his condition correctly. More amazingly still, he decided to treat him with a new, recently discovered drug, an antibiotic called at that time M&B – a sulphur drug. My father was in hospital for a week and miraculously recovered. The doctor was a good German whom my father never forgot.

The winter of 1938 was severe and many prisoners suffered terribly. Clothing was inadequate and the men were forced to work in freezing conditions without proper protection against the cold. My father later told how (incongruously) he was able to subscribe to the Nazi newspaper the 'Völkischer Beobachter' which was quite a thick publication and which he and other prisoners wore under their jackets as quite effective insulation against the cold. This scurrilous newspaper had, ironically, at least one useful purpose.

An incident during this severe winter deserves mention. One morning during December the men were working outside the camp, cracking stones. It was bitterly cold and an icy wind caused the temperature to feel even colder than it was.

Soon after the midday break there came an unexpected order to return to camp. Some prisoners hoped that those in charge had taken pity on them and had realised that to work in such freezing conditions was well nigh impossible. Not so. Two prisoners who had also been working in an outside gang had escaped. Roll-call took place earlier than usual and when the men were lined up the order came: "Tomorrow all prisoners in the outside gangs will search for the missing men and if they are not rounded up you will all be made to stand in the barrack square until they are found." Then instead of being dismissed as usual the order came again "Prisoners will stay lined up" The wind was icy, the temperature almost at freezing point. The men had little strength left after working most of the day in this weather and soon some became weak and sank to the ground. The hours passed, more men passed out and were left lying on the icy ground. Eventually, about three hours later the order to dismiss was given and the prisoners returned to their barracks to find their hot soup frozen and almost inedible – their only hot meal of the day ruined. The search for the escapees continued over the next four days with no result.

Despite an anxious wait to be lined up again in the freezing cold the order did not come. Men were relieved to be allowed to stay in the barracks for those four days while the search continued. The authorities felt it was better to keep the prisoners indoors while the search went on. Also it was clear that the men could not work effectively in temperatures below freezing as it now was. This brief respite was a blessing for the weaker men who were able to recover some of their strength. But as always it was a case of survival of the fittest.

In the whole time of his incarceration my father survived because he was a fit man. Even at the age of 42 as he then was, his experiences of mountaineering, and skiing had kept him in excellent physical shape. He was able to endure where others weakened and went under and he never lost the will to survive and never lost the hope of eventual release.

He and the other prisoners often discussed the aims and objects of concentration camps, vainly endeavouring to trace a logical design behind the concept. It was clearly understood that political enemies must be suppressed and even tortured and killed but then why did they intern innocent non-political men of all classes. Why Jews, gypsies and homosexuals some of whom were treated better than others? Why were some prisoners allowed to die of their illnesses and others, such as my father treated well? It gradually dawned on the men that the lack of system was the system. The greatest torture of all was the uncertainty. They did not know why they had been arrested, did not know when or even whether they would ever be released, did not know when one or other of their torturers would pick on just one man. That was the system. Another uncertainty the prisoners had to deal with was the possibility of war. Strange as it sounds the thought of what would happen particularly to the Jews exercised their minds whenever rumours of war circulated. Would they immediately be shot – a definite likelihood. Perhaps they would be forced into the front line and ordered to dig trenches, another ingenious possibility furthered by the barrack orderlies. They also baited the prisoners with remarks such as "when the war breaks out you Jews will have absolutely nothing to be amused about." A twisted malicious joke made by these unintelligent and vicious men.

In November and December 1938 some prisoners were beginning to be released. On what principle these releases occurred was a mystery but my father continued to hope. By January the releases increased. It was said that those whose relatives had made arrangements for their emigration overseas were allowed to go but many including my father who had arrangements in place were still there. Some who had no such arrangements were released.

When the loudspeaker in the barracks square began to blare forth the names of the lucky ones it was said "the parrot is drawing numbers again." The reference being that at fairs in Germany parrots were used to draw lucky numbers out of containers. My father's name was called at the end of February, but almost immediately his hopes were dashed. The camp was put in quarantine because of an outbreak of typhoid fever. Releases would cease, it was said for three months. However it was only six weeks before the releases were resumed. My father's turn came in April. Along with twelve other prisoners they began the long and involved process to freedom.

First a shave, not only of the face but also of the head. Then a trip to the hospital where they had to strip before being examined for marks of ill-treatment such as bruises or weals. Any prisoners who bore such marks remained in the camp until the marks disappeared. Next, to the clothes store where they were required to strip again, retaining only handkerchief and purse which was carefully examined in case secret notes (diaries and tales of the atrocities for instance) were being smuggled out. The authorities left nothing to chance. Then they were led into a room where surprisingly, the prisoners found their own clothes lying on a table. These had been carefully cleaned after the trip from Vienna to Dachau, so that all traces of blood and other unmentionable stains had been removed. The clothes hung loosely on the prisoners since most had of course lost a considerable amount of weight. Then they were marched into the Commandant's office where they received any money left in their accounts. At the gate, as a last bizarre episode they were faced by a barrack's officer holding a collecting box for "Winter Help" The officer saw to it that a fairly large amount was placed in the box. They were then marched out of the gate for the last time. At the Gestapo office just outside the main gate, they were addressed by an SS officer. He spoke clearly and with a certain menace, "You are now free. Do not in any circumstances say anything about the camp you are now leaving. If anyone asks, you can tell him to come and see for himself. If you do talk about what is happening here you will be returned instantly, together with your wife and family. Be aware that there is a camp for women and children as well as for men. Any one of you who returns to a concentration camp for any reason will not leave it alive. I also warn you to say nothing if you are travelling abroad. We have agents all over the world and if any atrocity stories are told by anyone he will soon see what happens to him and to his family. Do you understand?" The prisoners understood only too well. My father's comparative silence over many years could have stemmed from these gruesome words which were only too believable. Men who had witnessed the workings of the camps could easily imagine the worst outcome of all, wherever they might be in the world.

Next the men were called into an office one by one and given release passes. They were required to sign a declaration that they were well, had suffered no harm and had no claim against the authorities. It was also required that an undertaking be given not to repeat anything at all about the camp and its workings. Even a man who had lost his left hand in the camp signed only too eagerly. To get out as quickly as possible was the only thing on their minds. Everyone signed of course. Then the prisoners boarded an omnibus sent from Weimar. They were accompanied by a barrack officer as far as the Weimar railway station where he suddenly and strangely vanished. Here they were met by a committee of ladies who helped the men to obtain tickets, food and cigarettes as well as sending telegrams to relatives in Austria or Germany. The train arrived and the men entered the carriages – all was normal. They could hardly believe it.

My father had been a captive for 11 months. He arrived in Vienna where his mother and sister waited – had been waiting for all those months. From his mother's apartment he immediately telephoned my mother in Manchester. She lifted the receiver and one can only imagine her feelings when she heard my father's voice at long last. The next step was the immediate gathering of documents to facilitate the leaving of Vienna as quickly as possible, before, God forbid, my father was arrested once more. My grandmother, who was to go to England with him already had her passport and visa ready. My aunt was to stay in Vienna to arrange the collecting and sending of my parent's possessions to their eventual destination. My father although he had a passport, needed an entry visa for England. For this document he was required to apply in person. He told the following story many times.

He arrived at the British Consulate late on a Friday afternoon, knocked on the door and was told that the ambassador had already finished for the day and would not be at work until the following Tuesday. To lose three days at this time could have been disastrous – their flight to London was already booked for Monday. My father had in his possession a letter, which had been sent from London to his sister. It came with a personal introduction to the British Ambassador. It also contained details of his incarceration. He thrust the letter at the man at the door and asked him to at least show it to the ambassador. With trepidation he waited, a long wait for the man who had waited so long for release from not one but two hell holes. Quite soon the door re-opened and he was shown first into the hall of the consulate and then immediately into the office of the Ambassador.

'Nothing could have been stranger for me at that time' said my father. 'I entered a different world.' He saw a book lined office, beautifully and comfortably furnished with Persian rugs on the floor and sitting at his desk the picture of the perfect Englishman in tweed jacket and tie, a moustache and in his mouth, a reassuring pipe. He shook hands with my father and asked him to sit down in an easy chair. In this unlikely environment my father was finally able to relax. Over a cup of tea he told the ambassador his story. An hour later he had his entry visa. After his dreadful experiences this piece of civilised life was wonderfully heartening. There were still compassionate and understanding people in his world.

On arrival in Manchester, with his family around him the experiences of the last eleven months retreated somewhat. He was healthy despite the weight loss and with good food and, at last, a proper bed he relaxed and became well again. He and the family made expeditions to the Welsh mountains and even climbed Snowdon – another mountain to add to his list of climbs.

In July 1939 my father, mother and I embarked on the Orient Liner Otranto for Sydney. The necessary papers for entry into Australia had come through before their applications to emigrate to America or New Zealand.

We arrived in Sydney two days before war in Europe was declared. The ship docked at Woolloomooloo where the wharf has been completely refurbished. Luxury apartments and fashionable restaurants now exist where refugees with hope in their hearts disembarked in 1939.

A new life was beginning.

...

Top: Ernst shortly after his release.
Bottom: List of clothing, money and keys returned on his release.

The passport that took Renate and Fritzi toEngland.

G.8491/52536　　　　　British Passport Control Office,

Wallnerstrasse 8,

Vienna 1,

6th.March, 1939.

Mrs. Fritzi Raubitschek,
15 Sandy Lane,
STRETFORD,
Nr. Manchester.

Madam,

With reference to your letter of the
27th February, I enclose, herewith, an official
form requestion your husband to forward his
passport to this office, on receipt of which he
will be granted a visa for the United Kingdom.

Yours faithfully,

Passport Control Officer, Vienna.

GPB.
Enc.1.

The vital document allowing Ernst's entry to the United Kingdom.

Fritzi and Ernst Raubitschek on his arrival in England.

Afterword

Life began again in earnest. It was not an easy time for my parents, intent on making their way in this new and strange world, intent on re-establishing themselves. We lived first in a flat in Rushcutters Bay. Our belongings, those that still remained in Vienna had been sent to Sydney in what in those days was called a 'Lift.' Probably an immense packing case. In this retrieval we found many strange things, odd pieces of furniture such as one dining chair, 3 beds with horsehair mattresses, a Persian carpet and various common kitchen implements. (I still use my grandmother's wooden spoon, its handle wasted, after so much knocking on the sides of saucepans.) The packing of the lift had been organised by my industrious Aunt Fritzi – working on our behalf again. It was a pity that most of my father's wonderful library was left behind as was my mother's piano. I suspect that my Aunt believed that Sydney, being at the very end of the world would lack the bare necessities of life and had packed accordingly. However most sensibly, she had sent all of my father's dental equipment, which arrived intact and was put to immediate use. He set up a surgery in the back room of the flat and soon found patients, mainly of course amongst the many fellow refugees living at Kings Cross. He practised on 'the black', as it was called, because his Viennese qualifications were not recognised in Australia. Undaunted he applied and was accepted at Sydney University as an undergraduate to study for his degree in Dental Surgery. My mother found work as a dress designer. Thus I, being rather in the way as it were was sent to boarding school – to the Marist Sisters at Woolwich as a weekly boarder. Renate Raubitschek, the new girl at the convent was a novelty. 'What is your name?' I was asked.

'Renate …'

'No I mean your Christian name …'

This particular exchange dogged me throughout convent, high school and university by which time I was so used to the ritual I could do it in my sleep – the explanation, the spelling, the respelling of both names. I was never sorry that my father did not change our surname as so many other refugees did, mainly for convenience sake but shedding at the same time the name part of their individuality. I was only proud that he did not. At home we spoke German. I did not turn against the language as so many children of the refugees did, understandable no doubt especially during the war but nevertheless in the end a loss for them. My parent's English improved rapidly. When he began his Dentistry course, my father's English had been rudimentary, a handicap he soon overcame. He passed all his exams (in English) without one failure. Books, in English were purchased constantly and both my mother and my father read avidly, a dictionary always beside them. Later I benefited greatly from their choices enjoying many English classics.

In Vienna my parents had been great and enthusiastic sportsmen, skiing in winter and mountaineering in summer – stories of their adventures I have told earlier. Upon their arrival in Sydney they immediately began to explore the countryside. Every weekend they walked or hiked. At first only for the day, later for whole weekends, camping amongst the strange foliage, sleeping under new stars. They got to know and love the bush as well as they had known their beloved Wiener Wald.

At the University my father made many new friends, amongst them some keen horse riders. His experiences in the Austrian Cavalry had made him into an expert rider and although my mother had never ever been on a horse's back she decided to give it a try. Under my father's tutelage she soon learnt the art and in the end loved riding as much as my father did. As soon as I was old enough, I too was taught to ride by my father. We hired our horses in Wentworthville, then a totally rural area, where one of my father's University friends Ralph, kept his horses. Ralph's mother was an expert rider and I remember her riding a beautiful pony stallion, as black as boot polish and as shiny. I rode a tough little brown shetland called Lady Jane, who gave me a lot of trouble until I learnt how to handle her. We rode across paddocks, green hills and dirt roads to a farm called 'Tally Ho' near Rouse Hill, run by two maiden ladies who gave us wonderful afternoon teas. I have not forgotten their delicious tomato sandwiches and their plump scones with strawberry jam and thick cream. Later we often spent summer holidays at the Chalet, Mt Kosciusko where we explored the Alps on horseback. We rode over the whole main range to the Summit as well as across the Snowy river as far as the Blue Lake. Sometimes we rode all the way down to the Thredbo River, quite a long way from the Chalet and at the end down a very steep descent to the river. While we rested the horses, the men would fish for trout making for a delicious dinner that night.

George Day, who was the manager of the chalet in those days caught the wild Brumbies which had to be broken in for tourists such as us to ride. Often my father would help him. One day he was riding a horse which bucked quite ferociously but did not manage to unseat him. A small boy who was watching said 'Mummy, is that the Man from Snowy River?' I loved it all, we rode for miles and neither the heat nor the flies bothered us at all.

During the week my life was at school. The nuns were kind but found it difficult to cope with the small foreigner. I could read very well but had never been to school before so there was much to learn – not only academically but socially as well. I talked too much, I was too inquisitive, I did not like the food and said so – I did not fit in as I should have. I well remember the look of dismay on Sister Gertrude's face when I asked her the meaning of the words 'Immaculate Conception'.

During the war the school was evacuated to Mittagong where the nuns were building another convent. The structure was incomplete though it did have bedrooms on an open veranda and a dining room. The school cat would often join me in bed, creeping under the covers and keeping us both warm. For lessons we had to go down the road to a small house which had been bought for that purpose – to fill in until the main building was complete. I remember morning tea there being either bread and jam or bread and dripping both of which we all loved. Because of the fear of bombings, trenches had been dug in the school grounds and we had great fun playing in them. Fortunately they were never used for the purpose for which they had been built.

At the outbreak of war my parents had been declared enemy aliens. In order to visit me at Mittagong they were required to go to the local police station and fill in a form requesting permission to travel. This applied even to travel to another suburb and thereby hangs a tale. By now we had moved to Lindfield, away from the Cross as my father was at the University full-time. My mother, who was a keen musician and a very good pianist was much in demand for chamber music groups and on this occasion had been invited back to the Cross for an afternoon of music at the home of a Doctor, an Ear, Nose and Throat Specialist. For this trip she required a permit and dutifully got off the train at Chatswood, walked down to the police station (it is still there) and although having applied for the permit three days earlier was flatly refused. Permits were not issued for 'pleasure'. My mother explained that she needed ear treatment but the officer was adamant. Seething with fury now she decided to travel without it. The moment she boarded the train she realised that a detective was following her and sure enough at Wynyard he declared himself and went with her. In the tram on the way to the Cross she attempted to explain to him the difference between Germans and Austrians and how Austria was annexed by the Germans but he had no idea about any of the recent events in Europe nor was he in the least interested. Arriving at the Doctor's door my mother burst out with 'Doctor I am here for my ear appointment …' to little avail. The Doctor had answered the door with his violin under his arm. Soon afterwards she received a summons to appear in court and was fined five pounds with two pounds extra for the detective – a large sum in those days.

However permits for travel to Mittagong were allowed and my parents came to visit me as often as possible since school holidays were restricted, again because of the war. Instead, one recreation devised by the nuns was a walk into Mittagong on Sundays after mass so that we could spend our pocket money at the local lolly shop. My favourites were aniseed dumbells, peanut toffees and rainbow balls which intriguingly changed colour as one sucked, necessitating the removal of the sweet from the mouth quite often to check on its colour.

My father obtained his Bachelor of Dental Surgery Degree in 1943 and then worked for two years at the Dental hospital as his contribution to the war effort. No longer was he an enemy alien. He subsequently opened his own dental practice on the Pacific Highway in Lindfield. He soon became a very successful and much loved dentist on the North Shore, over many years treating whole families, their children and their children's children.

At this time we lived in a flat at Wollstonecraft while I went to North Sydney Girl's High School. As the practice flourished my parents decided to buy a block of land in order to build their own house. They found what they were looking for in Livingstone Avenue Pymble. It was a steep, bushy block on which stood many large and beautiful gum trees. Higher up and away from the road the land flattened out and was an ideal spot to place a house.

They employed Hans Oser, an architect with modern views who, amongst others favoured open plan living and flat roofs. Building was begun in 1948 when such enterprises were extremely difficult to bring to fruition. First of all there was a limit on the size of the house, overcome to some extent by the building of a large veranda over the garage which became almost another room. Building materials too were hard to come by and so work proceeded very slowly. I remember my parent's delight when they at last obtained a bath only to have the builder drop a hammer into it thus smashing the precious commodity beyond repair. It was months before they obtained another one. We moved into the completed house in 1950 and my parents lived there all of their lives. It was an innovative house, with an L shaped living room which sported an unusual fireplace open on two sides which my father doubted would work. However it did work and worked magnificently, warming both the sitting and the dining areas equally. In winter it was my father's greatest delight to light his fires, either the one in the living room or the one out in the garden where he burnt the multitudinous leaves dropped by the eucalypts.

With my mother's enormous interest in music it was natural that I would learn to play an instrument. I began to study the violin at the convent and went on to be a pupil of the well-known Russian violin teacher Jascha Gopinko who had been in Sydney since the early twenties and had built up quite a reputation. He was a lovely man who chain smoked, his overflowing ashtray on the side of the piano as he taught. Often he upbraided me when I hadn't practised by saying sternly 'today you're just up to putty!' I enjoyed playing for many years despite feeling faintly ridiculous carrying the instrument to school. I did find a young man who courageously carried it for me for a time, regardless of the sneers of his schoolmates as they passed us in the tram.

The matter of food was a subject much discussed by most refugees when they first arrived in Sydney. During the war there were ration books and coupons for many basics and my mother often exchanged her tea coupons for butter or coffee. The Jewish dietary laws were kept by very few refugees in those days. In fact we knew none who did. What would the Viennese do without their pork and ham? A story doing the rounds went like this –

Man in the delicatessen shop to the girl behind the counter pointing – "Would you please give me some of that chicken?"

"But Sir, that is ham."

Man outraged – "Did I ask you?".

Many of the foods the Viennese were used to were unavailable and not only because of the war – at that time they simply did not exist. It would take time and many more immigrants to make a difference. There was one man who made various types of continental sausages at home and came to my father's surgery selling them from a suitcase. He later became one of the biggest smallgoods manufacturers in Australia.

When I decided to study dentistry at Sydney University my father was delighted since I would be the third generation of the family to do so. I enjoyed my time at the University and practised for some years before giving it up in favour of writing. My father was not disappointed. In fact he was most encouraging as he enjoyed writing essays and research papers himself.

He was very pleased when one of my short stories was accepted for 'Coast to Coast', a collection edited by Leonie Kramer. It was very sad for me that he did not live to see my novels published.

After I graduated my parents took me back to Europe for a long trip. We went to Italy first, then to Vienna of course. My mother's mother was still living there and pleased indeed to see her family after such a long time. My mother had invited her years before to come to live with us in Sydney but she refused. She was perfectly happy, living with her companion of many years, enjoying summers in the country, winters in Vienna and wanted no part of a strange new country whose language and life she did not understand. I was introduced to much that my parents had experienced in their youth, not only in Vienna but also in their beloved mountains and lakes. It was a wonderful trip and I gained almost a stone in weight indulging for weeks in the most delicious foods imaginable. I was even persuaded by my father and my uncle to climb a mountain with them both – the Hochwilde in Austria (4000metres high). It was quite an exhilarating and of course exhausting experience for me. My parents left me in London where I spent some years working and travelling until I returned to Sydney to get married. It was a small quiet ceremony with a reception devised by my father in the garden at Livingstone Avenue. My husband and I bought a small cottage in Turramurra where we lived with our two children for some years before we moved to the country.

In 1971 my father suffered a stroke. He hated being incapacitated having been a healthy active man until then and lived, bedridden, mercifully I privately thought, only three months before a final heart attack.

After Tim and I built our house at Cobbitty in 1973 and began our country life I often thought of my father and how much he would have loved to join in with our new experiences. We had many horses over the years, the children learnt to ride at Pony Club, Emily winning jumping events and eventually Nicholas playing polo. For this Nicholas was able to wear his grandfather's long riding boots which had also arrived in the lift – two pairs – both from his cavalry days, one brown and one more elegant pair in black. My father would have been inordinately proud to see his boots on the polo field.

What on earth was my aunt thinking as she packed those boots. I sometimes wonder.

...

21 Livingstone Avenue, Pymble.

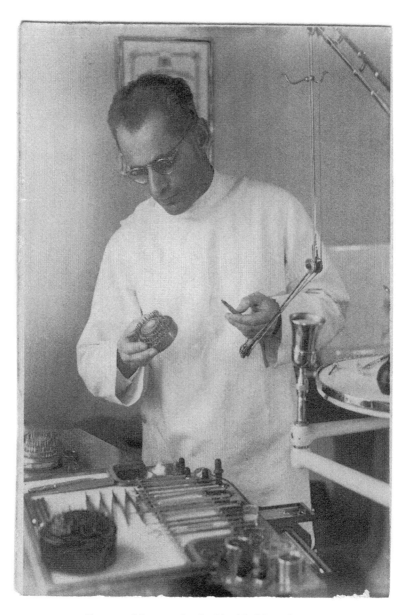

Ernst at his practice in Lindfield, Sydney.

Ernst and Renate, Sydney.

Renate and Ernst at 'Tally Ho' Farm.

Ernst and Renate crossing the Snowy River.

Top: Polo match at Cobbitty Polo Club. Nicholas riding Polly and wearing Ernst's boots. Emily at the truck holding Shannon.
Bottom: Emily and Shannon, nicknamed by the family 'The Wonder Horse'. He could jump, event, cross-country and play polo.

Ernst at Mount Kosciusko.

Printed in Australia
AUOC02n2126031215
272184AU00002B/6/P